W9-BZW-664

Mozart

Story by Jan Weeks
Illustrations by Mark Wilson

Harcourt Achieve

Rigby • Steck-Vaughn

www.HarcourtAchieve.com
1.800.531.5015

PM Extensions
Ruby

U.S. Edition © 2013 Houghton Mifflin Harcourt Publishing Company
125 High Street
Boston, MA 02110
www.hmhco.com

Text © 2005 Cengage Learning Australia Pty Limited
Illustrations © 2005 Cengage Learning Australia Pty Limited
Originally published in Australia by Cengage Learning Australia

All rights reserved. No part of this work may be reproduced or transmitted in any form or by any means, electronic or mechanical, including photocopying or recording, or by any information storage and retrieval system, without the prior written permission of the copyright owner unless such copying is expressly permitted by federal copyright law. Requests for permission to make copies of any part of the work should be addressed to Houghton Mifflin Harcourt Publishing Company, Attn: Contracts, Copyrights, and Licensing, 9400 Southpark Center Loop, Orlando, Florida 32819.

12   1957   18
26516

Text: Jan Weeks
Illustrations: Jan Weeks
Reprint: Siew Han Ong
Printed in China by 1010 Printing International Ltd

Mozart
ISBN 978 0 75 789229 5

Contents

CHAPTER 1

The Stray

The first time I saw her I was on my way home from school. I was walking along eating what was left of my school lunch when I suddenly caught sight of her. She was sniffing around the bottom of the garbage can in front of Wilson's shop.

She was the shaggiest, dirtiest, most neglected little cat I'd ever seen.

"Come here, girl!" I said, as I held out the meat from my sandwich. But she shied away, preferring not to accept my gift even though we both knew she wanted it.

"Suit yourself," I told her as I pushed the meat into my mouth. "Go hungry! See if I care."

I might as well have been talking to myself because the cat was no longer there. She'd disappeared into the bushes at the end of the street.

The cat reminded me of the Persian cat we used to have. Mops had been like a member of our family. We'd all loved her. That's why it had hurt so much when she'd run out on to the road, and then, suddenly, we didn't have her any more. Dad had offered to buy us another cat but, after Mops, nobody seemed to want another one.

I met the stray cat again, the next afternoon. She was back at the garbage can, still looking for something to eat. I didn't have anything to give her this time, but it didn't stop me from kneeling down, hoping to get her to come closer.

"Come to James," I said, but it didn't do me any good. With a wary eye cast in my direction, she ran off again into the bushes at the end of the street.

The next day, I saved one of my meat sandwiches to give to the cat, but there was no sign of her. She's probably found a better hunting ground, I thought – but I was wrong.

I saw her again the following day, but now she was limping.

I also noticed that the garbage can had a new lid on it. Maybe the cat hadn't had anything to eat all day. This time when I held out the slice of meat, she didn't run away. Instead she stood looking at it, licking her lips, as if trying to decide whether or not to take it.

To make it easier for her, I dropped the meat on the ground and then stepped back to let her know I meant her no harm.

"I know you're hungry, girl," I said in a soft voice, trying hard not to scare her. "Come and get it," I coaxed. "I won't hurt you."

Still looking at me, she inched her way forward, until at last she had the food in her mouth. In one gulp it was gone. Then I watched as she licked the spot where the meat had been.

"Poor little thing!" I said, wishing I had something else to give her. "You *were* hungry, weren't you?"

Hoping that she might let me look at her leg, I stepped closer. But, using the three good legs she had left, she backed away.

"Maybe next time," I said softly.

CHAPTER 2

A Kitten, Too

"Would you like another cat?" I casually asked Mom later that night. We were all sitting together at the table eating a fish dinner.

"Not really," she answered.

"I'd like another cat," said Madeline, my little sister. Then she started getting excited. "I'd like a great, big, fluffy cat just like Andrew's."

Andrew was our cousin, and he had a brown tabby. Every time Madeline went near that cat he knocked her over – so I couldn't really imagine why she'd want a cat like him.

"So how come you're asking about a cat?" said Dad.

"Oh, no reason," I answered, shrugging my shoulders.

It was then that Mom noticed I hadn't finished my dinner. "Eat your fish, James," she said. "You've hardly touched it."

"I'll eat it," Madeline said quickly.

"You won't like it," I told her. "It has bones in it."

Then, before anyone could say anything else, I took my plate into the kitchen. I was saving the fish for the stray cat. I had decided I would give it to her on my way home from school the next day.

That next afternoon, the cat was waiting at the front of the shop again. This time, when I offered her the fish, she ran straight to it. She even let me stroke her fur as she was eating it, although I was careful not to touch near her face. I guessed it was a long time since she'd had a really good meal.

Having eaten my food, the cat stood still and, this time, she let me look at her leg.

I saw right away what the problem was. She'd stepped on a splinter of wood and it was sticking out between the pads on her back paw.

As gently as I could, I pulled the splinter out.

She glared at me and gave me a sharp sideways look. For a second, I wondered if she might lift her paw to scratch at me. But she didn't.

Instead she walked casually back toward the bushes at the end of the street. Then she stopped and turned back to look at me. When I didn't move, she took a few more steps, then turned again.

"What's the matter, girl?" I asked. "Do you want me to follow you?"

The cat walked on, stopping every now and again to look back and see if I was following her. We went into the bushes at the end of the street and walked on until we came to a hollow log. It was well hidden among ferns.

"So this is where you live," I said, as I watched her disappear inside the log. "Thanks for inviting me, but I'm too big to crawl in there."

A few seconds later the cat came out again. In her mouth she was carrying a small, dirty brown bundle. It was a kitten! A tiny ragged-looking kitten. It didn't look very old, I guessed no more than a few weeks.

The cat carefully dropped her little kitten at my feet and sat down. For a while I didn't do anything – just watched them. Then I reached out and gently touched the kitten. The cat didn't seem to mind, though she did keep watching me. When I felt sure she trusted me, I picked the kitten up and held it against my chest. It was just so beautiful – and so fluffy and soft! I wondered if there were any more kittens in the log, but the cat didn't go back in. She just stood there, looking at me, as if waiting for me to make the next move.

"Come on, girl," I said finally. "I'm going to take you both home."

CHAPTER 3

Taking Them Home

Mom was digging in the garden when we came home. She stopped what she was doing to look at us coming through the back gate. "Look, Mom, they're Persian cats – just like Mops," I said, trying to win her over. And I might have, too, if the cat hadn't chosen right then to have a good scratch.

"Except that she's covered in fleas!" Mom answered. "And she's dirty, as well."

"I'll get her a flea collar," I promised, still hoping she'd let me keep them. "And the kitten is really cute. Look!"

Unable to resist puppies or kittens, Mom reached out her hand to take him. As she cradled the kitten in her arms, I explained how I'd found them.

"They don't have anywhere to live," I told her. "They're hungry and they're cold." I knew it was summer, but I thought it still sounded convincing. "Can they come and live with us, Mom? When Mops got killed, Dad *did* say we could have another cat."

"Please, Mom! Let them stay!" pleaded Madeline, who had joined us by now and had already taken the kitten from Mom. "They won't eat much, and I'll help to take care of them, too."

"It could be that they already have a home," Mom answered.

I shook my head. "I'm sure they don't," I said.

"Strays don't usually wear a collar," Mom explained, reaching down to show us the one that was around the cat's neck.

I hadn't noticed the collar before, probably because it was buried under all her fur.

When I asked if the collar had anything printed on it, Mom nodded. There was no address or phone number, only the cat's name: *Princess*.

"Maybe her owners didn't want her any more," I said, hoping that was true.

"Or it might be that she's a lost cat," Mom answered.

"So that means we can keep them," Madeline decided, already carrying the kitten toward the house.

"Not so fast," Mom called out. By now Madeline and I were half way to the back door.

Then Mom's face softened as she looked at the tiny kitten in Madeline's arms. "I think there is some flea powder in the cupboard, left over from when we had Mops," she said. "But neither of those cats is allowed inside – not until they've both had a good bath. Then you can make them a bed in the laundry room."

I didn't mind. In fact, I was thrilled! For the moment, it was enough that she was going to let them stay overnight.

One at a time, we put the cats in the laundry tub. Princess didn't like being washed and kept trying to jump out. But she didn't once try to scratch us. With her coat cleaned and brushed, she really did look a lot like Mops.

"I had no idea she was almost white under all that dirt," Mom said. "She's really quite pretty, isn't she?"

Dad thought so, too. "Mmmm," he agreed. He was sitting in a chair holding the kitten.

Early the next morning, I woke to the sound of piano music. At first, I thought it was Madeline playing her toy piano. But when I went to investigate, I saw that it wasn't Madeline at all. Someone had left the laundry room door open and the kitten had found his way out of the laundry room ...

It was the kitten that was playing the music, walking up and down on the keys of the toy piano. It sounded awful!

"Regular little Mozart, isn't he?" Dad laughed.

"That's a good name for him," I said. I'd been trying to think of one. "We can call him Mozart, after the famous composer and musician who lived a long time ago." I knew all about Mozart because our teacher had talked about him at school.

CHAPTER 4

Newspaper Notice

Dad loved animals, and I knew if it had been up to him, he would've let us keep both cats. Mom was the one we had to convince. She'd been especially sad when we lost Mops. Mops had been *her* cat – a birthday present from Dad.

"They won't be any trouble," I promised. "I can even use my allowance to buy their food. And I'll clean up after the kitten. I'll do anything to keep them," I begged.

"It's not a good idea for us to become too attached to them," Mom answered. "We'll just be disappointed when their owner comes to claim them."

As if that was going to happen! It didn't take long for that to change, though. When I followed Mom into the kitchen, I heard her making a phone call.

"The cat is a white and ginger, female Persian," I heard her say. "She looks about two years old, and has a tag on her collar with the name Princess on it."

"What were you doing?" I asked, shocked, when Mom hung up the phone.

"Talking to someone at the newspaper," Mom answered. "I've arranged for a notice to be placed in the lost and found column."

"Why?"

It was a silly question. I already knew the answer. It was to see if they could find the people who owned Princess and Mozart.

"Putting a notice in the paper is the right thing to do, James," Mom said. "There could be a family out there who are very upset to have lost their pets."

I knew she was right, but that didn't make it any easier.

"They can't have Mozart," Madeline said. "If anyone comes, I'll hide him."

"Okay, then," Mom said. "If the cats aren't claimed, we can keep both of them. Maybe we'll be lucky," she added.

The newspaper came out three days later. By then we'd become even more attached to Princess and Mozart. I jumped every time the phone rang, thinking that it might be the cat's owner trying to get in touch with us. I was so relieved every time it wasn't.

CHAPTER 5

Being Brave

After a week went by and we still hadn't heard anything, I began to feel more confident.

"I told you Princess was a stray," I said to Mom.

But I hadn't realized that notices in the local newspaper run for two weeks. I guess that's why I was so surprised when I came home from school one day to find that Mom had something to tell me.

And I could tell, by the look on her face, that it wasn't something I wanted to hear.

"Did someone call?" I asked. I could actually feel the color draining out of my face.

Mom nodded. "A man is coming to pick up Princess and Mozart at four o'clock this afternoon. Apparently he had been visiting his grandchildren and hadn't seen the first notice in the paper. He said Princess is a very valuable cat. She was stolen over three months ago. Since then the police had tried to find her but with no luck. The man said that he hadn't known Princess was going to have a kitten."

Madeline was sitting at the table. "I don't want him to take Mozart," she cried. He was her favorite. Mine, too. It didn't seem fair. Not after ten days of *living* with us! Mozart was part of *our family*!

"We are going to have to be brave about this," Mom said. Then she told Madeline it might be best if she stayed in her bedroom when the owner came. She was upset enough already.

"Princess must have escaped from the person who stole her," I said. "She must not have been able to find her way home."

"Which explains why she was so dirty and hungry," Mom answered. "Poor little thing! She must have had her kitten inside that hollow log."

At exactly four o'clock, a car pulled up at the front of our house. I watched through the window as a man climbed out. The minute he saw Princess, his face lit up. She ran straight into his arms. The man told us how grateful he was that we'd taken care of his cat.

I knew then that Mom had done the right thing placing the notice in the paper. Even so I still felt sad to see him taking Princess and Mozart away. Our house was going to seem so empty now without them.

The man's car got as far as the end of the street and then turned around.

"He's coming back," Madeline said, now out of her bedroom.

The man stepped out of his car and walked back toward our house. In his hand, he was carrying Mozart.

Madeline and I rushed to open the door.

"I think you should keep the kitten," he said, smiling.

Now it was our turn to be grateful to him.